THE LAW: FROM PRISON TO THE STREET

Mark Nicholson, Esq.

By: Mark Nicholson

Jacobs & Whitehall
73-03 Bell Blvd, #10
Oakland Gardens, NY 11364
www.jacobsandwhitehall.com

Ordering Information:

Quantity sales. Special discounts are available on quantity purchases by corporations, associations, and others. For details, contact the publisher at the address above.

Orders by U.S. trade bookstores and wholesalers. Please contact Jacobs & Whitehall: Tel: (888) 991-2766 or visit www.jacobsandwhitehall.com.

Printed in the United States of America

Published in 2022

ISBN: 978-1-954506-62-6

PREFACE

This book is about certain rights people have in prison and on the street. It is not my memoir, but I talk about some of my past. It is not a comprehensive analysis of the law. This book is for people incarcerated or that have loved ones incarcerated. Also, it is for those interested in the law and the curious public to glimpse some rules and regulations that people face in prison and on the street.

Many people are unaware of their rights, and sometimes the government violates our rights. I hope this book helps brings awareness about prisoners' rights and the rights of those of us on the street.

DEDICATION

I dedicate this book to Gina and our children. My mom, Donna, and dad Marion Nicholson. My sisters Becky, Tina and Mary. The late Professor Mary H. Mitchell. And my best of all friends, James Coatie.

ACKNOWLEDGMENTS

I want to acknowledge a few of the many people that have helped me throughout my journey in life. My high school teacher, Roger Miller. Jessie Cook, my criminal defense attorney. My FBF, Kristen Reese, for helping me get a job with the Indiana State Public Defender. Courtney Benson-Kooy for being the best trial partner I have ever had. Attorney Angka Hinshaw for being a good leader. Deidra Haynes and Finis Tatum for pushing me into private practice.

Judge Ken Johnson for hiring me and allowing me to work for him. Justice Frank Sullivan, Jr., for introducing himself to me and giving me good advice. Attorney Jon Laramore for all his support.

My good friends from prison, Kevin P., Dwayne P. and Alvarnez M.

Finally, I want to acknowledge a few organizations that helped me. Hoosier Veterans Assistance Foundation (HVAF), Horizon House and Indiana University McKinney School of Law.

DISCLAIMER

This publication is intended to be used for educational purposes only. No legal advice is being given, and no attorney-client relationship is intended to be created by reading this material. The author assumes no liability for any errors or omissions or for how this book or its contents are used or interpreted or for any consequences resulting directly or indirectly from the use of this book. For legal or any other advice, please consult an experienced attorney or the appropriate expert who is aware of the specific facts of your case and is knowledgeable of the law in your jurisdiction.

Law Office of Mark Nicholson

www.marknicholsonlaw.com

(317) 667-0718

9702 E. Washington Street

Suite 171

Indianapolis, IN 46229-2609

TESTIMONIALS

"I can't thank you enough Attorney Mark Nicholson. I hope to see you again in New Castle Indiana representing clients in need of a good attorney with professionalism as yourself. Mark you did an outstanding job for my friend in the court room. You were always available through phone or email with quick response. I was so impressed with your professionalism, as we know Lawyers are important advocates whom represent us through the legal system. Mark I think when people read your profile, it speaks for itself. This is a hardworking, professional attorney that cares about his clients. Thank you."

— ***Gail***

****

"Mark represented me a couple of years ago. I had a drug possession case and we had a jury trial. He fought very hard the entire trial. The jury returned a not guilty in 30 minutes! I walked out of the courtroom and haven't been back."

— ***TJ***

****

"During my initial hearing Mark came up and introduced himself to me. He was very polite and seemed very professional and gave me his card. I contacted him later that day and we scheduled a consultation. We set up an easy payment plan that would work well for me. At court he was able to make sure that I got the bare minimum and explained everything to me since this was my first offense. I would recommend Mark to anyone! He did an amazing job and if I ever need an attorney again, it will definitely be Mark."

— ***Anonymous***

****

"I was introduced to Mark Nicolson by my best friend to see about getting my record expunged. Mark took down my information and called me back the next day. I met him, paid my fee, and he did exactly what he said he was going to do. He doesn't just take your money; he's a sincere lawyer. I would recommend Mark Nicolson in a flash and would use him again if I needed an attorney."

— ***Stephanie***

****

Table Of Contents

By: Mark Nicholson

My Background

I was born and raised in New Castle, Indiana. Home of the world's largest and finest high school gymnasium. The gym is so big it could fit the entire county in it. I am joking about that, but it is big. New Castle is small, and I wanted to leave town as soon as I could. So, eight hours after my high school graduation, I left for the United States Army. I wanted to make a career of being in the military and lead men into battle. Of course, back then, they thought only men could be in battle. It took decades for the government to realize that women had been in every battle a man ever fought.

My battlefield experience came with Operation Just Cause. The invasion of Panama. General Manuel Noriega was the de facto Panamanian leader. The United States wanted him for racketeering and drug trafficking. Although, there is certainly more to the story than that. You do not invade an entire country to arrest one person on some drug charges. Well, in this case, we did.

After returning from combat, I had about a month of service left with the Army. Then I was going off to college. Indiana State University accepted me and I was going to be in their ROTC program.

Change and circumstances had other plans for me. It was February 3, 1991, and I was involved in a barroom brawl that left one person shot dead and another seriously wounded. The State of Indiana charged me with murder and I had two trials. The first trial ended with a hung jury in Vigo County. My attorneys filed a change of venue and my second trial was in Vanderburgh County, cause number 82D02-9210-CF-0443. The trial ended on November 21, 1992, and the jury convicted me of voluntary manslaughter and criminal recklessness. On January 22, 1993, the judge sentenced me to thirty years in prison.

Behind the walls of the prison, I never thought that I would be a lawyer. In prison, I was what they called a Lay Advocate. I was the person who represented people when prison officials accused prisoners of committing violations of the disciplinary procedures.

Prisoners received a “write-up” (technically, a Bad Conduct Report). I was pretty good at representing prisoners, even though I considered the Conduct Adjustment Board one of the most corrupt and unfair decision-making bodies in the country. When I won a case, they would call me Johnnie Cochran, and when I lost a case, they called me Johnnie Cockroach. Of course, it was behind my back, but I overheard some fellow prisoners calling me Johnnie Cockroach. It is hard to win a case when the guards find drugs on your client, and he admits it was his.

The Case the ACLU Refused to Take

The prison officials at the Indiana State Prison refused to allow me to have a newspaper called *Maoist International Movement Notes* (MIM Notes). I wrote the American Civil Liberties Union-Indiana (ACLU) with the hope and expectation they would take my case. Unfortunately, I received a very polite letter from an attorney named Ken Falk declining to take my case. He believed there was no way this would be a winner of a case.

I was disappointed but impressed with his honesty. I wrote a letter telling him it disappointed me they wouldn't take my case, but I understood. So, I set about the business of finding out what I needed to do to sue these folks for me to get the newspaper.

I went to the law library to begin my research. I always enjoyed going to the law library because it was such an educational experience. It made me feel equal to the people that had the job to put me in here. I could read the same thing they were reading. My understanding was just as good as theirs, I believed. I mean, the law is what it is, right? Well, until you get to law school. Then you learn that the law is a lot of "it depends."

After several weeks of research and preparing my documents, I sued the Indiana State Prison and Indiana

Department of Correction on September 7, 1999 under cause number 46D04-9909-SC-002495.

The filing was in the Laporte County Superior Courthouse. I requested a change of judge because I had heard that the judge normally wasn't fair to prisoners in his courtroom. I had a previous case in front of him against the prison, and he ruled in their favor without giving it a second thought. Looking back many years later, maybe I didn't even have a case. I don't know. I just know that I felt I was being treated unfairly and the word in the prison was that his court was bad news for prisoners.

He granted my change of judge. Maybe he did not want to deal with me again. They transferred the case out of Laporte Superior Court 4 and into Laporte Superior Court 2, 46D02-9911-CP-000166. The process really made me feel like I was doing some lawyering.

First, the opposing party was a real lawyer, Keith C. Norwalk, from the Indiana State Attorney General's Office. I heard he was an excellent attorney and had great success defending the Indiana Department of Correction against prisoner lawsuits. Some prisoners told me he never lost a case in State court and only lost a couple in federal court. I didn't know if that was true or not and really didn't care. I knew I had a good case, and that was all that mattered.

The Hearing

The hearing was originally scheduled for March 30, 2000, at 10:00AM. It was apparently rescheduled because the court did not issue a transport order. The next date for the hearing was April 26, 2000, at 1:00PM. They scheduled it for two hours. I thought that seemed like a lot of time to argue about something that should be a no-brainer. This time, the court issued a transport order.

It was the first time I had been out of the prison walls in a long time. I knew some prisoners would file all kinds of lawsuits and do or say anything to get out from behind the walls. I could definitely understand that, especially if you were never getting out of prison. It's easy to want to do whatever you can to get away from these 40-foot walls.

This lawsuit was not about just trying to take a field trip from prison. I honestly believed they were wrong for confiscating my newspaper. There was no legitimate reason for them to withhold it and if I could get before a neutral court, they would surely see that I was right.

The afternoon of the argument was a nice sunny day. I remember being shackled like an animal, hands and feet. They transported me in a prison van. The courthouse seemed like it was just around the corner. The ride took around 30 minutes, but it sure went quick. There were no windows in the back of the van, so I really couldn't see where we were going or what was on the outside. I don't remember getting a taste of the outdoors. I just remember being able to see out a window inside the courthouse and the front windshield of the van.

When I was inside the courtroom, my opinion changed. I felt prepared, but overwhelmed. I didn't believe the government attorney could come up with a rational explanation of why I couldn't have the newspaper. But, I thought, they did not need to a have a rational explanation. The judge was in his robe, the government attorney in his suit, and the guards with their weapons. I felt out of my element, all alone, and that I had no chance.

I presented my argument and had plenty of copies of previous *Maoist International Movement Notes* to display as exhibits. I wanted the court to know that I had been receiving them with no problems. Every issue always had letters from prisoners.

It never mentioned the prisoner's name, only the state they were in. "This issue, your Honor, had a letter from "An Indiana Prisoner." It was actually my letter, but I didn't think that made a difference. It didn't mention my name, and it wasn't a threat to the "safety and security of the prison," in my opinion.

But the government attorney had a different opinion. He argued that MIM Notes posed a clear and present danger to the "safety and security of the prison." I could never figure out his logic about how this issue threatened the safety and security of the prison. Other than there being a letter from "An Indiana Prisoner," and I seriously doubted that they knew the letter was from me. It just sounded like a bunch of lawyer speak and the judge was speaking the same language. I knew then that I didn't stand a chance and I would never get this issue of MIM Notes, and, from now on, I probably would never receive another issue.

After the court carefully listened to both sides of the argument, the judge said he would take the case under advisement. Although I felt the court listened to the government's side a little closer than mine, I was happy that the court didn't issue an opinion right then. I expected the court to issue its opinion, right on the spot, and in favor of the government. So, I wasn't sure what the court meant by taking it "under advisement" but I figured it must be something good because it didn't issue a ruling in favor of the Indiana State Prison.

On May 3, 2000, the Court issued its ruling. I remember being called to the counselor's office. The counselor's office is where we had to go to pick up our legal mail. I was not sure why I was being called there but I thought, "I've been pretty good lately, so this shouldn't be another, I'm in trouble visit to the counselor's office."

When I arrived at the counselor's office, the counselor he told me I had legal mail. I knew it was from the court and not an attorney because I had nothing else going on. I was a little nervous when I slowly opened the letter, but I was about 90% sure the court would deny me my newspaper. It wouldn't be the first time a court had denied me something, and I was sure it would not be the last. I didn't read the order in the counselor's office. I just opened it to show the counselor that there wasn't any contraband in the envelope.

I ran back to my cell and sat on my steel cot. Now I took the time to read, slowly, the court's order. The court ruled in my favor. I do not recall the actual language, however, the Chronological Case Summary states,

"Court now enters Judgment For plaintiff: The July 1, 1999 issue of MIM Notes shall be held by this Court for (30) days to permit Defts.' right to appellate review; if review is sought the issue of MIM Notes shall remain part of the appellate record; if review is not sought, Jdg. matter will be forwarded to Supt Anderson for delivery to Plaintiff."

I won! I could not believe it. Yes, I knew I had a good case. But I was not totally convinced that the court would rule in my favor. I thought there would be too much temptation to just let the DOC get their way. But this court, this judge, did what was right and followed the law.

My fellow prisoners told me I should go to law school when I got out. I did not have an interest in going to law school, nor did I think I had what it took for law school. I did not believe a law school would accept someone like me, a Black man convicted of a felony. Not just any felony either, but a violent felony. There is not a law school in the country that would give me an opportunity, especially in Indiana.

On November 4, 2002, they released me from prison. Although I had lost some good time credit, I gained it all back. Also, I earned my bachelor's degree while in prison, resulting in a reduction of my sentence. I was homeless, and it was cold in November. My first job was working with the American Civil Liberties Union of Indiana (ACLU). Technically, it was not a job because I volunteered. I received no payment for my work, and that was alright by me. I wanted to help people.

I sorted through the mail, and they received a ton of mail. It was like everyone in Indiana that believed someone violated their rights contacted the ACLU. I do not think people knew how small their office was in Indiana. There were about three to five attorneys, and they covered the entire state. The office was not large either. However, their passion for fighting for the rights of people was enormous.

Shortly after working with the ACLU, my friend Robin put in a kind word for me to get a job with the Citizens Action Coalition (CAC). I had my interview, and the interviewer asked me about my background. She already knew about my past.

Robin told her about it, and she was understanding. I interviewed to be a phone canvasser, and I got the job. I was a volunteer at the American Civil Liberties Union. The work I did at the CAC was for pay. It was my first paid job.

Angel Story

One day, I rode the city bus (the number 8) to downtown Indianapolis. It was a cold November morning, and it was snowing. I was on my way to work at the American Civil Liberties Union-Indiana. When I got off the bus and started walking, a man was standing on the corner, passing out flyers and shouting.

"Help homeless vets! Help homeless vets! Help homeless vets!"

People ignored him and walked right past him like he was not even there. As I approached him, I found out why people were ignoring him. He wanted donations.

I stopped.

"Hey, I'm a homeless vet. Will you help me?"

He said, "Yes."

He gave me his name and a phone number.

"Call this number and mention my name," he said. "They will get you housing and off the streets," he said.

When I arrived at the ACLU, I told Ken Falk, the director of the ACLU, about my situation. I told him I would go after work. He encouraged me to make the call right away and do whatever I needed to do.

I made the call to the Hoosier Veteran's Assistance Foundation (HVAF) and mentioned the person's name. They told me they didn't have anyone working there by that name.

"Matter of fact, we've never even heard of that name before."

"You have to know him. Maybe he wrote his name down wrong or something. He was passing out flyers downtown," I said.

That's when the HVAF representative gave me the sad news. "We don't have people passing out flyers downtown."

The man downtown tricked me.

"But we can definitely help you if you are a veteran," he said. I went from grief to gladness.

The HVAF representative told me what I needed to do and who I needed to meet with to get the ball rolling. He said that on certain days they have outreach workers at the Horizon House. Today was the day someone from HVAF was at the Horizon House. As luck (or GOD) would have it, the Horizon House was right next door to the ACLU. I gave Ken the update, and he told me to head on over to the Horizon House immediately. I did what he said and signed into the Horizon House. The Horizon House is a day shelter. It does not have bed space, but it has other facilities and services to help people that are homeless. There are bathrooms, showers, washer and dryers. If you're homeless, you can use their address to get your mail delivered there. They have a contract with local service providers that offered medical and mental services. They even provided job training services.

I waited for my turn to meet the HVAF representative at the Horizon House. His name was Michael Williams, and he had a lady named Cindy from the VA hospital with him. They interviewed me for about an hour. They asked questions about my background and how I got to be where I was. I thought they would tune out when I told them the Department of Corrections released me from prison about two weeks ago. It didn't turn them off; actually, they seemed genuinely interested and concerned for my well-being.

Mike and Cindy told me about the program and what was required. There was a curfew, and no drinking or drugs allowed. I had to agree to participate in a treatment program. My concern was if my parole officer, Steve King, would allow me to move into their transitional housing so soon.

I contacted my parole officer and told him what I wanted to do. He was all for it. I must have had the best parole officer of all time, or at least one of the best. It was easy to work with him. I never felt he was out to get me. I felt like as long as I wasn't causing him any trouble, he didn't care what I did. Anytime I spoke with him, I always felt like he wanted me to do well. He made me feel like he thought I wasn't supposed to be in the criminal justice system.

In a matter of a week or so, I would move into the Arlington House. I look back on that incident and think of it as my Angel Story. The man on the street was like an Angel to me. No one else seemed to pay him any attention. Just another person downtown trying to run some money scam. It was like the other people walking by didn't even see him. He was not meant for them. He was meant for me.

Go to Law School

In May 2003, while still working for the CAC, I made a phone call that would change my life. I spoke with a donor, and he asked about my background. I gave him the edited version, not telling him about my recent release from prison. "It seems like the law is in your background. Have you thought about being a lawyer?" he asked.

"No, it's too expensive," I replied.

Over the weekend, it was like God put it on my heart to go to law school. I didn't know anyone who graduated from law school; in fact, the only attorney I knew was the one who represented me, Jessie Cook. But I woke up the next morning with a mission and a passion for making the connections I needed to get into law school.

As soon as I could, I talked to Ken Falk, the man who still allowed me to volunteer my time at the ACLU. I asked him whom I should contact to make my way into law school.

“Professor Mary Mitchell is the person you need to contact,” he said.

He told me how she was such a fantastic person and would do whatever she could to help me get into law school. Professor Mitchell was so instrumental in helping me get accepted into law school. I was homeless during the first two years of law school. I lived on the streets and eventually found myself in a veteran’s homeless shelter. Hoosier Veteran’s Assistance Foundation (HVAF) was the organization that helped get me off the street.

Unfortunately, Professor Mitchell died unexpectedly on November 4, 2009. It was the same year that I passed the bar, and they swore me in as a lawyer. It was seven years to the day of my release from prison. And my son was born less than a hundred days later, on February 4, 2010.

Being accepted into law school and graduating was a dream come true for me. The first year of law school, my classmates voted for me to be their class president (i.e., Class Represeντive). My last year of law school, my classmates voted for me to be their graduation speaker. It was a pleasure and honor to get to know such brilliant people.

My First Jury Trial as an Attorney: The Battery Man

The case was called the Big Buford Battery case. Marion County prosecutors charged my client with throwing a Rally's Big Buford cheeseburger at the manager. The incident occurred at the drive-thru window. Then my client came through the drive-thru window, and an altercation occurred. It resulted in my client being charged with battery and strangulation.

They captured the entire altercation on surveillance video. The verdict was not guilty. The legend of Mark Nicholson, The Battery Man, was born.

Serving Time

I served my time in the military and in prison. Now I am serving my time as an attorney, helping people. I am a People Helping Lawyer known as the Battery Man because of my focus on representing people charged with battery cases.

What Was Prison Like?

No one wants people to mistreat them or to treat them like they are less than human. Prison is a very dehumanizing space; the guards try to break you down. They do not want you to have any confidence in yourself. The goal is for you to depend entirely on them.

Then, somehow, when they release you from prison, society expects you to be independent.

When I was in the military, they told us, “We’re going to break you down and build you up!”

The military wanted to turn me into an independent thinker, I thought. Actually, they tried to break the independence out of me, too. They just wanted to instill confidence, not independence. There was a chain of command we had to follow; orders we had to obey. But prison was all about breaking us down, stripping us of any confidence, and making us follow their rules without question. I had a hard time adjusting to that mentality because I never wanted them to institutionalize me. Being “institutionalized” means you take whatever the institution tells you and cannot think for yourself.

My independence and smart mouth led to the guards beating me. The first time guards abused me was at the Vigo County Jail. I was the only Black man in the cellblock. The cellblock held about twenty jail inmates. At some point, the White inmates did not want me in their block. So, someone, or maybe several of them, told the guards I was stealing their food and bullying all nineteen of them. The guards came and moved me out and put me in a solitary cell. When I asked them why they put me in solitary, the guards shoved me and hit me in the stomach. For the next sixteen months, I was in solitary confinement. A jail deputy named Jay helped me survive. In my memoir, I will talk more about him.

After my conviction and serving several years at the Indiana State Prison, they transferred me to the Indiana Youth Center. Correctional Officers at the Indiana Youth Center threatened to hang me from a tree, called me nigger, and placed me in solitary confinement. The only way that I could fight back was through the grievance procedure. The grievance board comprised three prison staff and one prisoner, and they ruled on all grievances filed within the prison. When I was at the Indiana State Prison, I wrote so many grievances that the board would only laugh at me and deny them. I did not stop because I believed that the only way to fight against this travesty of justice was by continuing to write these grievances and work as a Lay Advocate. I did not expect that this would prepare me for my legal career.

As a Lay Advocate in prison, I was like an attorney, writing grievances instead of motions. I worked in the prison law library and conducted research for my fellow prisoners, even the men on X-Row (Death Row). I was drafting Post-Conviction Relief (PCR) petitions for people before I became an attorney. Now, I write PCR Petitions as an attorney and get paid in cash instead of food from commissary.

CHAPTER 1

IN PRISON: ENCOUNTERS WITH GUARDS

What Are the Common Types of Encounters That Prisoners Have with Guards?

The most common type of encounter a prisoner will have with a guard is during searches. Cell searches, they called them "shake-downs," were when the guards searched a prisoner's cell. The guards were always searching a prisoner's cell, looking for contraband, weapons, and drugs. Or they searched prisoners when they entered the church, the recreation area, visits, or anywhere else. The search and discovery of contraband probably led to the most prison rule violations.

What Are Some Major Issues and Infringements on Prisoner's Rights?

The main issue that prisoners experience—whether in federal prison, state prison, or even county jail—is the invasion of privacy. There is not any privacy in prison. You eat, sleep, shower, and defecate in front of everyone. In that environment, prisoners have essentially no right to privacy at all. It is difficult to transition from a society where we protect privacy to a world where guards can enter your space and conduct a cell search or even a body cavity search at any given time.

Another infringement is the freedom of association. They scrutinize the mail coming in and even out of prison. They interfere with contacting your family, access to magazines or books coming in and out of prison, and access to your attorney. The rights we often take for granted on the street are limited in prison. Prisoners have limited First Amendment rights, too. Sometimes, prisoners have their rights to freedom of religion, freedom of speech, and access to their attorney violated.

Another common issue is the cruel and unusual punishment that occurs in prison. Examples of deliberate indifference in prison are the lack of adequate healthcare and the physical brutality guards inflict upon prisoners. Cruel and unusual punishment results in frequent prison lawsuits. Prisoners are often physically and mentally abused by correctional officers. When that happens, prisoners or their relatives claim the government violated their civil rights. The alleged violation is based on cruel and unusual punishment.

CHAPTER 2

ENCOUNTERS WITH LAW ENFORCEMENT ON THE STREET

What Situations Commonly Lead to Encounters with Law Enforcement?

Driving, walking, and being accused of a crime are the most common encounters people have with law enforcement. Cases commonly called Driving While Intoxicated (DUI); in Indiana, it is called Operating a Vehicle While Intoxicated (OVWI). It does not take much to think of examples of someone driving while under the influence of drugs or alcohol.

Police are always alert for those types of drivers. Intoxicated drivers are usually easy to spot, making them a prime target for law enforcement encounters.

Of course, the police consistently encounter people that drive over the speed limit, do not signal a turn within 200 feet, or engage in other traffic violations. Once the police stop you, if they smell the odor of marijuana or see drugs in plain view in your vehicle, then they can ask you to step out of the car while they search it. If you illegally possess drugs, then your day goes from bad to worse.

As you can see, there is a similarity between encounters with law enforcement in prison and on the street. A similar issue is a search. Getting searched by the police can lead to some unfortunate circumstances. One reason that interactions between African- Americans and police are tense is that both parties are scared. The bottom line is that although officers may be well-trained, most of them are scared. Most police will not admit to being scared, but they are, and it is understandable. They have heard stories of encounters with civilians that ended in the officer getting killed. If you are an African- American, you might also be scared because you have heard of so many encounters between police and African-Americans. The Black man ends up being killed by the police in your story. The police officer is the one who gets killed by the Black man in their story.

In many areas—especially in low-income African-American communities—the police patrol the streets and then stop people they see on the road. Sometimes it may not be consensual, but the officer will justify the stop as a consensual *Terry* stop encounter. A *Terry* stop is also known as a stop and frisk search. The *Terry* stop name is from the U.S. Supreme Court case called *Terry v. Ohio.*

Basically, a *Terry* stop is when a police officer has a reasonable suspicion that an individual is armed, engaged, or about to be involved in criminal conduct. The officer may then briefly stop and detain an individual for a pat-down search (frisk) of outer clothing. A *Terry* stop is a seizure within the meaning of the Fourth Amendment of the United States Constitution.

CHAPTER 3

RIGHT TO REMAIN SILENT

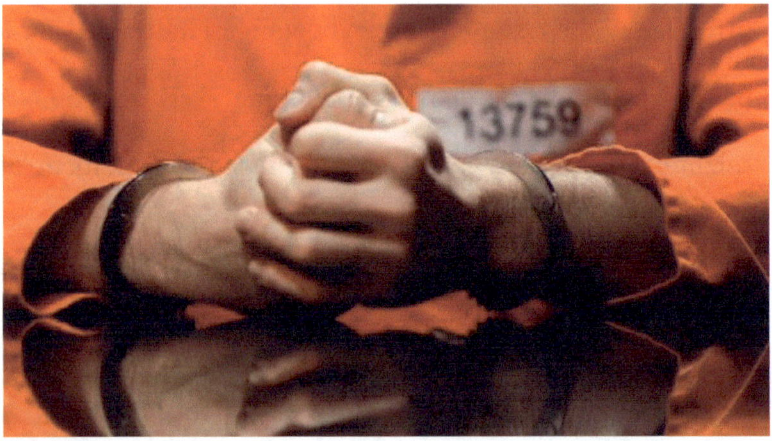

What Are the Common Scenarios of a Prison Guard Questioning Prisoners?

The most common scenario when a prison guard questions a prisoner is when they are trying to get information about what is going on in the prison. Their questioning is understandable; they would argue because the safety and security of the prison is paramount. The guards want to know who is bringing in drugs, who is selling the drugs, who is assaulting people, and trying to plan an escape.

They want to engage with prisoners they think are going to snitch. The word snitch has been around for probably longer than the first prison built in the United States. There is a phrase that prisoners use when referring to snitches.

"Snitches get stitches and get buried in ditches."

The prison staff and investigators listen to prison phone calls, and if they get an idea that a prisoner is committing a violation or if someone snitches on them, the guards will begin questioning prisoners about the activity.

For example, guards sometimes make it seem like someone was snitching when they were not. They would take a prisoner to the investigator's office and then bring the prisoner back to the cellblock or dormitory to make it look like the prisoner was snitching.

Sometimes, either during or after they bring the prisoner back, they would search for another prisoner. If they find any contraband, it would appear that the prisoner that just returned was the prisoner that snitched.

Why would the guards do this? They hope this will cause other prisoners to attack and kill the prisoner they think was snitching. They did it because they wanted to eliminate a prisoner they believed was causing them trouble.

Do prisoners have the right to remain silent? Yes, they do.

They can say, “I’m not talking to you. I’m exercising my right to remain silent.”

The key thing to remember is that they do not have to answer questions from the prison staff. The only thing that a prisoner should say is their name, Department of Correction number, and their prison location.

Prisoners do not have to provide any information that could incriminate them or others. I highly encourage them to remain silent. However, remaining silent can still carry consequences I will get into in a later chapter.

If a guard asks, "Did you see what was going on last night?" or "Are you aware of someone bringing in drugs?" or "Did you make some hooch (alcohol) over the weekend?" just don't answer.

Prisoners have a right to remain silent and not incriminate themselves, and technically, the guards cannot punish them just for that. In reality, the guards may try to retaliate. They may put the prisoner in solitary confinement or even physically beat the prisoner to get an answer. Of course, this is not proper, not something they should do, but they do it. It may not happen all the time, but once is more than enough.

Do Prisoners Have Access to a Lawyer When Questioned by Prison Staff?

Generally, no. There are many types of prison rule violations, such as failure to obey a direct order, missing Count Time. Count Time is when the prison staff counts the number and location of prisoners. If the prisoners are not where they are supposed to be when they are supposed to be there, then that is missing Count Time. Other prison rule violations are having an excessive amount of property, harming yourself, or harming someone else.

Some violations in prison mirror those on the street, but they do not always want to charge prisoners with crimes, so they have their internal disciplinary system.

For example, having unauthorized possession of state property might result in a theft charge on the street. In prison, a prisoner would face internal discipline. The sanction could range from losing privileges like recreation, phone, commissary, or visits to a grievous loss sanction. A grievous loss sanction means the prisoner loses their good time credit and has to do more prison time.

When a prisoner faces a violation of a prison rule, it does not entitle them to an attorney. However, the prison will provide them with a Lay Advocate. A Lay Advocate is a prisoner that represents another prisoner when the prison staff accuses the prisoner of violating prison rules. The Lay Advocate makes arguments on behalf of the prisoner they represent; they can call witnesses and cross-examine people, just like an attorney.

Prison staff will judge the accused prisoner. It is easy to imagine that the prison staff that wrote the Bad Conduct Report against the prisoner will probably be friends with the people sitting as judge and jury. However, depending on the offense, the prison staff may refer the case to the county prosecutor and the prosecutor charges the prisoner with a crime (not just a prison violation). If they send the case to the county prosecutor, the prisoner has the right to an attorney (for the criminal case) and the right to remain silent.

CHAPTER 4

RIGHT TO REMAIN SILENT ON THE STREET

During Encounters with Law Enforcement on the Street, Do You Have the Right to Remain Silent?

Most people have heard or seen TV shows where the police arrest someone and read them "their rights." It seems like it is a favorite or used to be a favorite on cop TV shows. I currently do not watch cop shows, so I do not know if they show that part as they used to when I was much younger. I cannot stand watching all the police violating the constitutional rights of suspects and always being right. It is a form of brainwashing or indoctrination that gives the police and the prosecutors an edge when they arrest someone. For example, even though people have heard about their Miranda Rights and the police train on it, too often, people either do not exercise their right to remain silent, or the police violate their right to remain silent.

Many people believe if the police ask you a question, you have to answer. Society trained a lot of us that way. When someone asks you a question, you give them an answer. It is rude not to answer, and you do not want to upset the police. I have seen cases where a person answered police questions or gave the police permission to search, even though the person knew they had something illegal on them or in the car. It never seems to end well. The police usually find the illegal items and arrest the person. Now, the prosecution has several advantages if the police conducted the search and questioning legally.

Regardless of whether the police did it correctly, the person should hire a lawyer who represents people charged with those types of crimes.

I like to say, "You don't tell a bricklayer how to lay bricks unless you're a bricklayer." If you are not someone who makes a living conducting interrogations and questioning, you will probably not do too well during an interrogation, and the police know that.

I always suggest exercising your Fifth Amendment right to remain silent. If the police are charging you with a crime, remain silent. If the police are investigating you for a crime, remain silent. Demand to speak with an attorney. They train many law enforcement officers in the Reid technique, which is an interrogation technique. This technique has resulted in false confessions, and some police departments are no longer using it. The police are very experienced in interrogations. You cannot beat them at their own game. It is what they do day in and day out. The facts show people continue to get convicted by false confessions. Do not talk to the police. Remain silent.

It is usually best to tell them, "I'm exercising my right to remain silent," and then get an attorney. At that point, they should stop questioning you until you have an attorney present. If you're on the street, you have a right to an attorney under the Indiana Constitution and the United States Constitution.

On the Street: When Does Someone Get Access to an Attorney When Being Questioned by Law Enforcement?

When you invoke your right to an attorney, the police should cease questioning you. They should allow you to get an attorney. I have had people call me while the police were at their house when the police pulled them over, and I have even spoken to the officer at the scene. Mostly, it is up to the officer's discretion to determine when you can contact your attorney. If they are in the middle of arresting you, they may not allow you to reach your phone and call an attorney. You may have to wait until after the police arrest you and process you through the system.

The bottom line is that you have a right to an attorney. Once you say, "I'm exercising my right to remain silent, and I want an attorney," the police can no longer ask you questions; their questioning is over. However, if they smell marijuana or have some reason to investigate further, they can order you to get out of your car, and they can search you and the car. The law (Miranda) allows you the right to not answer their questions. The police should not continue to ask questions about the incident once you exercise your right to remain silent.

If you are in your house and the police do not have a warrant, then you could just tell them, "I'm closing the door," and they cannot come into your house. Like most things with the law, there always seems to be an exception. If the police fear a crime is being committed or some other emergency circumstances, they could enter without a warrant and against your will.

Of course, there is plenty of case law that proves the police do not always follow the law. They violate people's Fifth Amendment rights (Miranda rights). When the police say, "You have the right to remain silent. Anything you say can and will be used against you in a court of law," listen to the police, if they ever tell you that. The police will use your words against you and sometimes even twist your words to make you look guilty. It is crucial to remain silent if you are being accused or investigated for a crime and do not have an attorney.

Once you invoke your Fifth Amendment Right, the police should give you access to an attorney. Do they always do that? No. Unfortunately, it is not as easy as calling an attorney to help you and the police immediately stop questioning you. Unless you have an attorney on standby, rarely does that happen.

Sometimes they just throw you in the cell, and you will have to call your family members when you have time to use the phone. Or you end up calling an attorney and letting them know you are in jail.

CHAPTER 5

SEARCH AND SEIZURE IN PRISON

What Are Some Common Scenarios That Lead to Search and Seizure in Prison?

In prison, you do not have the same rights to privacy as you do on the street. In state prison, nearly everything belongs to the state. It is all State of Indiana property. Since it is their property, they have the right to do whatever they want with their property. If someone is coming to visit a friend or family member in prison, the guards will search the visitor for contraband. The guards will search the prisoner before the visit, too. It is common practice for the guards to search prisoners before entering the gym, church, education area, work, and any other prison events. The prisoner has no right to resist the search. Prisoners have to let the guards search them for contraband. Of course, if the guard is harassing a prisoner or sexually assaulting the prisoner, then that is a different story. The guards also have the right to seize property for a variety of reasons. If they determine a prisoner has too much property or anything considered contraband, such as cigarettes, tobacco, and cell phones, then they can confiscate it. They can search the property of prisoners and restrict it if the prisoner is in disciplinary segregation.

There are two main types of prison searches: searching prison cells and searching the prisoner for contraband. Searching the person includes pat-down (or frisk) searches, visual or strip searches, urine testing, X-rays, and blood tests. Is it permissible for prisoners to be patted down by someone of the opposite gender? Yes, it is allowed, but that does not give the prison official the right to touch genital areas and breasts.

There are other types of searches, like the areas within and around the prison, prisoner work areas, recreation, religious services, visitors, and employees. Prison officials justify the need for searches because prisoners may try to escape, plan acts of violence, and sneak in contraband.

The right to privacy does not apply in the prison environment. The Fourth Amendment protection against unreasonable searches does not extend to a prisoner's cell. Prison officials may conduct cell searches to maintain the safety and security of the prison.

Prison officials may seize any items not allowed. See, *Hudson v. Palmer*, 468 US 517 (1984).

What Does a Prisoner Do If They Believe the Guards Violated Their Rights?

If a prisoner believes the guards violated their rights, their first step is to file a grievance. In most prisons across the country, there is a grievance procedure that they have to follow. It is an internal administrative mechanism that the federal and state courts want prisoners to exhaust before filing with the court. The next step is to report the violation to the Department of Corrections' central office in Indianapolis. If the prisoner does not like the result from central office, then the prisoner may file in federal or state court depending on the situation. The prisoner can also seek help through various legal organizations, including attorneys who represent people who meet specific criteria. The prisoner may look for an attorney to help them address the violation. In the federal Southern District of Indiana, the court may appoint an attorney. Not all people will qualify for legal help, but that does not mean they should not seek help.

What Is It Like for a Prisoner Who Is Fighting for Their Rights in Prison?

Most prison administrations do not want prisoners fighting for their rights. In part, they do not adequately train the prison staff to deal with that issue. They focus their training on how to deal with prisoners who physically fight back. I would imagine a sense of boredom to train perpetually on handling violent prisoners, but never having to handle violent prisoners. There is a sense of excitement and adrenaline rush when the prison calls for their tactical emergency response teams. Prisoners offensively referred to the prison's tactical units as the "Goon Squad." The reason they were called "Goon Squad" relates to the original goon squads that were a group of criminals or mercenaries to intimidate or assault others. Traditionally, they were used for inflicting violence on pro- union or anti-union groups.

The Indiana Department of Corrections has several emergency teams: a Quick Response Team (QRT), Emergency Response Team (E-Squad), Special Emergency Response Team (SERT), Canine Team (K-9), Situation Control Team (SITCON), and Critical Incident Stress Management Team (CISM). The members of these Emergency Response Teams may wear a lot of protective gear and face shields (as seen in the recent protests after the murder of George Floyd). These are some of the most highly trained correctional officers the Indiana Department of Corrections offers the State of Indiana. This is how they deal with physical resistance. When a prisoner writes grievances, it is often more challenging for the prison to respond with anything other than denying the grievance. It would be nice to have an emergency response team handle situations when the guards violate a prisoner's rights.

Is Solitary Confinement Humane?

Solitary confinement is not humane. They sometimes refer it to as "close management," "administrative segregation," "disciplinary segregation," or other names to draw attention away from the stigma of solitary confinement. Multiple studies show the detrimental effect of solitary confinement. I suggest reading the information published by the Southern Poverty Law Center (SPLC) and the American

Civil Liberties Union (ACLU) concerning the negative effects of long-term solitary confinement.

Solitary confinement can increase mental illness and exacerbate those who already have a mental illness. Being isolated for long periods diminishes social and emotional skills.

Look at how people reacted when we were quarantined in our homes during the pandemic in 2020. If people were stressed out because they had to stay home for a few days or weeks, just imagine the stress of being confined in an eight-by-eight foot cell for years.

The US Department of Justice found that juveniles in solitary confinement experienced paranoia, anxiety, and depression. Another research report found that most juveniles who committed suicide while incarcerated were in solitary during their incarceration.

By: Mark Nicholson

Are Conditions in Prison Improving?

They arrested me on February 3, 1991, and released me on November 4, 2002. They incarcerated me for approximately 4,293 days or 11 years, 9 months, and 2 days; or 141 months, and 2 days; or 370,915,200 seconds; or 6,181,920 minutes; or 103,032 hours; or 613 weeks and 2 days. I round all that up to say 12 years.

Things have changed since my prison time. There are modern amenities like tablets, email messages, Xbox and PlayStation, etc. However, some things will never change. The feeling of loneliness, the pain of losing your freedom and your privacy, feelings of anger, guilt, or resentment; those feelings will exist as long as prisons exist. Also, the violent nature of prison will always be there. It fluctuates with time, but prisons are not as violent as they once were. They are still not safe, but there are not as many mass prison riots and holding of hostages like there were throughout the 1970s to 1990s. Using solitary confinement and the Supermax prisons has contributed to reducing prison riots and mass casualties. However, there are exceptions to the rule. For instance, the homicide rate in the Alabama prison system has increased over the last decade (Report from the Alabama Department of Justice and the US Bureau of Justice Statistics, 2007–2018).

Prison litigation is less because Congress passed laws in the 1990s to make it harder for prisoners to sue and recover for prison abuses. A lot of the prison litigation that happened in the 60s, 70s, and early 80s was because attorneys could make money by representing prisoners and suing the prisons. However, the Prison Litigation Reform Act (PLRA) and Bill Clinton's Antiterrorism Effective Death Penalty Act (AEDPA) changed prison litigation and made it harder for prisoners to start litigation against prisons. It also reduced incentives for private attorneys to represent prisoners because it reduced the money they could recover. The law effectively prevented people that were being abused and having their rights violated from getting the legal help they needed.

While some creature comfort-related things have improved in prison, the dehumanization of prisoners continues, and the lack of human interactions still exists.

CHAPTER 6

SEARCH AND SEIZURE ON THE STREET

What Are Common Interactions with Police That Lead to Search and Seizure on the Street?

One of the most common interactions that leads to search and seizure by the police on the street is driving. If the police smell marijuana or see something in the vehicle that gives them a reason to investigate further, they can ask you to get out of the car. Then they can search.

Probably the second most common police interaction is while walking in public. In some areas, it is more common for the police to stop people while walking. It is less common for the police to stop a White person walking than for the police to stop an African-American male or Latino male walking down the street. This is something that African- American males and Latinos frequently face, or at least fear.

Under Indiana law, you have the right to walk away from an officer who asks you to come to the patrol car, but if they claim you are "running" away then they will have a reason to chase you and conduct a search and seizure. Also, they may arrest you for resisting law enforcement (resisting arrest).

Of course, another interaction that would lead to a search and seizure is being charged with a crime or arrested for a crime. For example, if your spouse calls the police for a domestic violence incident. In some circumstances, the police may enter your home. They may search you to make sure you do not have any weapons. The reason for this search is for the safety of the officer. Finally, if the police arrest you, then they will search you.

What Rights Do I Have on the Street?

On the street, you have the right to be free of unreasonable search and seizures. Often, police act on a hunch before they engage in a search, which is not legal enough. They train police to have reasonable suspicion and probable cause before engaging in a search and seizure. For instance, if the police pulled you over, they may claim that there was an odor of marijuana, even when there was not. The police will use that to take you out of the car and search the car, and sometimes you. This could be an unreasonable search and seizure because they had no reason to get you out of the car and search it. However, good luck trying to convince anyone that the police did not smell the "odor of marijuana" because all cops know that is the magic phrase in Indiana to start a search. When the police find marijuana in your car, they will say they smelled it, and that was why they asked you to get out of the vehicle and conducted the search. The stop may never show up on the radar of statistics if they don't let you go.

When an attorney believes that the search was illegal, the attorney can move to suppress the evidence by filing a motion to suppress. The judge could rule that the officer violated your constitutional rights and suppress the incriminating evidence because the officer did not follow the law in obtaining it. Unfortunately, there are some judges that have a reputation of never or rarely granting a motion to suppress.

CHAPTER 7

EXCESSIVE FORCE IN PRISON

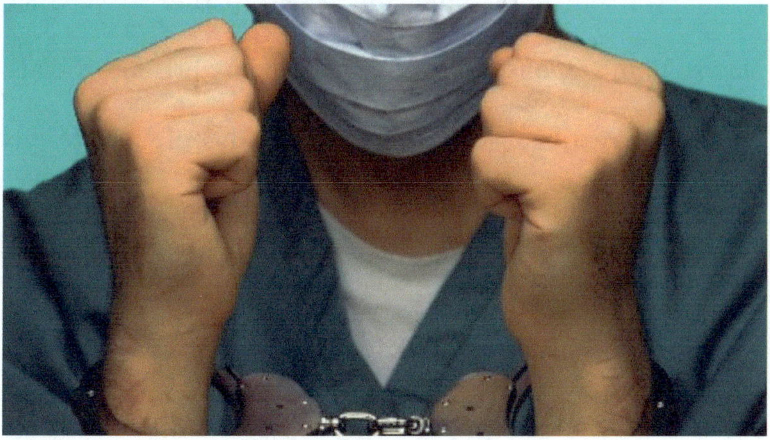

Does Excessive Force Occur in Prison?

Unfortunately, excessive force occurs in prison. In one instance, I witnessed the guards beat a prisoner so severely that a guard held each limb as they carried him out of the cell, blood dripping from his face onto the ground. When the prisoner's shoe fell off, a nurse jumped up in the air and stomped on his shoe like it was a pesky cockroach. I do not know why she did that, but I realized she must have let her personal feelings impede her professional duties. It was all too common for guards to engage in excessive force.

Prisoners or other interested parties have filed lawsuits in response to excessive force by prison officials. Some correctional officers have set people up to get murdered in prison. For example, if a prisoner threatens to kill another prisoner, instead of the correctional officers moving one prisoner to safety, they can keep them in proximity to each other.

The guards may place the prisoners in the same cell, hoping that one of them would kill the other.

Another typical example is when the prisoner informs the guard that he is afraid that his cellmate will rape him. If the guards do not protect the prisoner, then it is their responsibility for not taking action. Situations like this often cause lawsuits when correctional officers show deliberate indifference to prisoners' issues.

By: Mark Nicholson

What Kind of Training Do Correctional Officers Receive in Using Excessive Force?

I speak with the caveat: I have never been a correctional officer (CO), nor have I taken part in their training. However, I have witnessed some of their training, spoken to several prison officials, and researched some of their training.

Correctional officers all get trained, but the level of training differs. Some COs may have a military background, and some may be former or retired police officers. In most prisons in Indiana and throughout the country, the COs do not have guns or lethal force inside the prison. They usually reserve deadly force for the COs who are in the towers and not in direct contact with the prisoners. They train COs in using various weapons, including pepper spray.

The people on the "Goon Squad" supposedly receive a higher level of training that involves hand-to-hand combat, although they may call it combatives or self-defense.

When Is Force Excessive?

In some ways, it is a matter of just knowing it when you see it. In the landmark United States Supreme Court case on obscenity, *Jacobellis v. Ohio*, 378 U.S. 184 (1964), Justice Potter Stewart said although he could not define hard-core pornography, "I know it when I see it." Trying to define excessive force can be hard. Basically, excessive force refers to force over what an officer reasonably believes is necessary. They may hold an officer liable for using excessive force in an arrest, an investigatory stop, or other seizures of people.

But what is reasonably necessary? In most cases, the COs will justify their actions—just like police officers do on the street. The supervisor will support the CO or officer because they are all in it together. Sometimes, however, a CO will not get support for their use of force when it is so blatant that no one could defend it.

The question of the reasonable amount of force necessary is an issue attorneys must address when preparing to litigate these cases. Attorneys must listen to the facts, investigate, and research them. Litigating against prisons and the officials that run them is often very difficult because of their enclosed society. It is tough to get access to a prisoner, and prison officials can throw all kinds of roadblocks in your way to prevent access to the client or potential client.

Some people may think the prisoner is making things up to get sympathy or reduce their sentence. The bottom line is this: abuse happens, and sometimes there is a fine line between whether the level of force was excessive or necessary.

CHAPTER 8

EXCESSIVE FORCE ON THE STREETS

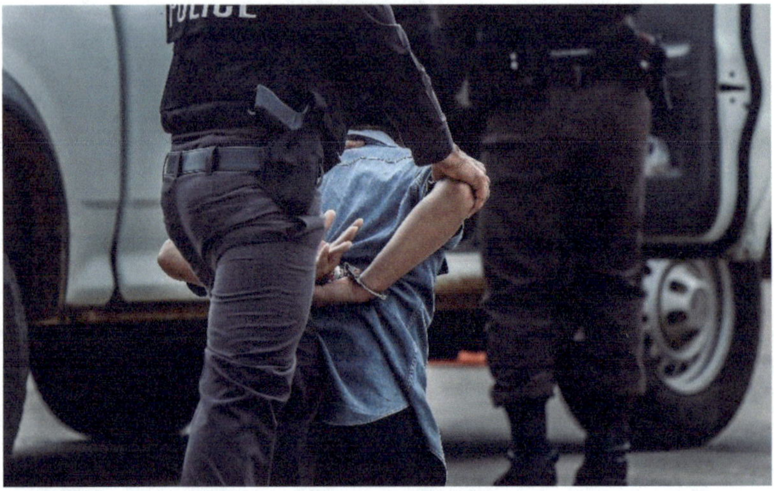

Does Excessive Force Occur on the Streets?

It seems like excessive force is being implemented by law enforcement more frequently than before. However, it is probably not more abuse than before, but the proliferation of cell phone cameras capturing the abuse live. A lot of what we see lately is not new to most African-Americans. We have lived with this basically since the beginning of being brought over here to this country. In my experience, the tool used by White supremacy and systematic racism is the abuse of police powers. If you look throughout the history of this country, the abuse of police power and excessive force has been used to stop people whom the police and politicians dislike. Look how it was in the 60s against African-Americans and other minority groups. I suggest people to research the FBI's COINTELPRO activities to gain a better understanding.

Things are changing. Instead of a bunch of Black people protesting against police brutality, there are a bunch of White people protesting against police brutality, too. After the killing of George Floyd, in some areas, more Whites were protesting than Blacks. In the 60s, it was the opposite. Blacks were protesting, and they had very few Whites protesting with them. More recently, prosecutors have charged officers with murder for killing unarmed Blacks. This is unusual because previously, they would not charge officers when there was a claim of excessive force. Prosecutors left it up to the victims or family members to sue in civil court.

Resisting arrest is another tactic police used to abuse their powers. Sometimes, when they falsely accuse people of resisting arrest, the officers will claim that is why the person has physical injuries.

In a case I had, the officer thought he turned the video off to save the battery. The officer said he was switching to audio-only. This was during an Indianapolis pilot program of body cameras, so the officer may not have known precisely how the camera worked.

Then he went into my client's house, grabbed her arm, and told her to quit resisting three times. My client was just standing there and was not resisting. But if you just heard the audio, you would have thought she was resisting. This is only one example of many when officers use resisting arrest as a vehicle to prove their actions were right or to teach a person a lesson, especially if the person asks a lot of questions, talks back, or gets smart with them and they don't like what the person said.

What Kind of Training Do Police Officers Receive in the Use of Force?

They train most police officers in Indiana at the Indiana Law Enforcement Academy in Plainfield, Indiana. However, there are satellite facilities in Fort Wayne, Bloomington, Indianapolis, Hobart, and Evansville. Part of the training involves the force continuum, which entails police officers determining whether a civilian is compliant or resistant and aggressive or life-threatening. The officer's actions should mirror the civilian's actions. The officer should not react aggressively if the civilian is compliant. If the other person does not escalate the situation, the officer should not. The officer should start with verbal commands if the person is being compliant. The next step is nonlethal force, such as the use of pepper spray, if the person resists or is acting aggressively. When an officer fires their weapon, that is lethal force. Lethal force should be the last resort and reserved for life-threatening situations.

No rule says an officer must start with verbal commands; the officer gets to decide, which is understandable. If someone is pointing a gun at the officer, you do not want the officer to start with soft physical contact. The officer may not have time to give a verbal command. In that situation, the officer might have to jump right to lethal force. In a split second, officers have to decide what they will use on the force continuum.

Officers should always try to de-escalate the situation, but sometimes the police escalate the problem by behaving in a certain way. They train officers in various techniques to teach them how to de-escalate situations involving mental health issues and other situations. Although officers sometimes engage in excessive force, I am not aware of officers trained to use excessive force. Unofficially, some police departments may turn a blind eye if an officer uses excessive force.

Who Determines What Is Lawful Force and What Is Excessive Force?

An individual who believes they have been a victim of excessive force can sue, and the judge or jury will decide if the officers used excessive force. However, police officers have some qualified immunity. Qualified immunity is a judicially created doctrine that shields government officials from being held personally liable for constitutional violations, like excessive force. It prohibits money damages under federal law so long as the government officials did not violate clearly established law. I do not believe officers should have qualified immunity. If officers were not immune to being sued, they might think twice before engaging in excessive force or other abusive behaviors.

To file a complaint of excessive force in Indiana, you must file a Tort Claim within a certain period, alleging that the officer engaged in excessive force (e.g., kicked you when you were down, beat you up, abused you, etc.). The police (and other officials) investigate and determine whether the officers used excessive force. If you do not get a resolution at this stage, you can sue in court because you have exhausted your state remedy. Failing to file a Tort Claim may limit your legal options.

CHAPTER 9

CHARGED WITH A NEW CRIME IN PRISON

If You Are Charged with a New Crime, What Are Your Rights?

If they charge you with an actual crime in prison, you have a right to an attorney, the right to remain silent, the right to confront and cross-examine witnesses, and the right to see the evidence they have against you.

These are the same rights anyone would have after being charged with a crime. On the streets, being accused of a crime differs from being accused of a disciplinary violation in prison. It is the local prosecutor or the federal government that will charge you with a crime. You will have a right to a trial by jury and a plethora of legal rights that help to ensure you receive a fair trial.

If they accuse you of violating the disciplinary rules, then prison officials will write the disciplinary report. The local prosecutor and the federal government will not have any role in that. However, they could charge you with a crime and for violating prison rules, depending on the violation. They do not consider that double jeopardy.

If You Are Charged with a Crime on the Streets, What Are Your Rights?

The first thing you should do—and I cannot stress this enough—is exercise your right to remain silent. Tell the police you are exercising your right to remain silent and that you would like an attorney. When an officer is trying to talk to you, ask them if you are "free to leave." If they say, "yes" then you should leave, and if they say "no" then you should ask if you are being detained.

Your response to being detained by an officer is to tell them you are choosing to exercise your right to remain silent and that you want an attorney. You should get in contact with an attorney as soon as possible. In the meantime, do not talk to the police.

CHAPTER 10

PRISON LITIGATION

Most prison litigations are civil and referred to as prisoners' rights. There are three main areas of civil litigation involving prisoners. The main three civil actions are Habeas Corpus, Torts, and Section 1983. They often referred to these as 1983 lawsuits.

Habeas Corpus

Article 1, Section 9, Clause 2 of the US Constitution explicitly provides habeas corpus action.

"The writ of habeas corpus shall not be suspended, unless when in cases of rebellion, or invasion, the public safety may require it."

In a habeas corpus action, the prisoner must file a petition asking for relief. This focus must be on the legality of imprisonment or detention. The relief sought is a release from incarceration or detention. The prisoner-petitioner files a petition against the entity- respondent (usually a prison or jail) holding the prisoner in confinement. In prison, the warden/superintendent is the named the respondent. In a jail setting, the sheriff is the named respondent. The court will order the respondent to show cause why a writ of habeas corpus should not be issued, and why the petitioner should not be released. The respondent's response is ordinarily due within a short period, such as ten days.

Three Types of Habeas Corpus

There are three main types of habeas corpus:

Habeas Corpus ad subjiciendum. This reviews the legality of confinement. It is the most common within prison settings.

Habeas Corpus ad prosequendum. This orders the custodian to bring the party to court for prosecution.

Habeas Corpus ad testificandum. This orders the custodian to bring the party to court to give evidence in a court case. The custodian is the prison or jail. They have to bring the party (the prisoner or jail inmate) to the court to give evidence. Habeas corpus actions are generally filed in the county or district court where the person is held. These actions are treated as an emergency because they are challenging the legality of a person's confinement.

After the court receives a response from the respondent, the court may dismiss the petition; the court can hold a hearing for more information or grant the writ of habeas corpus. Habeas corpus actions do not test the guilt or innocence of a person in custody, nor are damages awarded in these types of actions.

The legal provision to seek habeas corpus relief is under 28 United States Code Section 2241 and 2254. Also, there is the Antiterrorism and Effective Death Penalty Act (AEDA) that amended habeas corpus requirements. This law placed limitations on the use of habeas corpus. Senator Bob Dole introduced the bill, Congress passed it, and President Bill Clinton signed it in 1996.

Under the AEDA, some of the new requirements were prisoners had to exhaust their state remedies before filing in court. It allowed the federal courts to dismiss an application for a writ of habeas corpus, finding the writ has no merit and established one year of limitation for prisoners to file a motion attacking the legality of their sentence under habeas corpus. The AEDA puts strict restrictions on the ability of prisoners to file a writ of habeas corpus. The constitutionality of the AEDA was challenged, but the Supreme Court upheld the law. See, *Felker v. Turpin*, 518 U.S. 651 (1996).

CHAPTER 11

STREET TIPS

Street Tips During Police Stops

Here are a few tips for interacting with the police during stops. For some people, being stopped by the police can be very stressful and scary. You may think you might not survive the encounter. You may know of stories about the police violating someone's rights or, worse, taking their life unlawfully. I hope the following tips can help you if the police stop you.

If the police stop you while walking:

Ask, “Am I free to go?” If they say yes, then slowly and calmly walk away. If they say no, then ask, “Why are you stopping me?” The police should answer but be prepared for a witty remark or no response.

If the police stop you while driving:

Show your license, registration, and proof of insurance. Keep your hands on the steering wheel, where the officer can see them. Before moving your hands, ask the officer for permission. For example, “May I reach for my wallet? May I get my registration from the glove compartment?” This should reduce the chance of the officer misunderstanding your movements and shooting you “accidentally.”

If they gave you a ticket that requires you to sign it, read it (if possible) and sign it. This can help reduce them saying you refused to sign and adding some other infraction or criminal charge.

In Indiana, if they ask you to take a Standard Field Sobriety Test (SFST), you are not legally required to take the test. Of course, the officer will not be happy and may even threaten you. If they ask you to take a breath test and you refuse, then you are facing serious consequences. They can automatically suspend your license because of implied consent. Implied consent means that you consented to take such a test when you applied for a driver's license and drove on the roadways. Finally, they can request a blood draw. If you refuse, they can seek a court order to draw your blood.

If the police arrest you, ask if you can have a licensed driver to get your car. In most cases, they will say no, but depending on the situation, they may say yes.

For further information on what to do if law enforcement suspects you of operating a vehicle while intoxicated, visit my website, marknicholsonlaw.com. Or go to Amazon.com and buy my e-booklet titled, *Accused of an OVWI? The Answer to 7 Questions You Need to Know.*

If the police ask you questions:

Exercise your constitutional right to remain silent. Tell the police, "I am exercising my right to remain silent." You cannot be arrested or detained for refusing to answer questions, but you should identify yourself if asked. In Indiana and other states, there is such a crime as refusing to identify. If you exercise your right to remain silent, make sure you do from the very beginning. The police will not appreciate the fact you remain silent, and they will be even more upset that you answer some of their questions, but not all. Either way, they will find your conduct suspicious, so just let them know you are remaining silent from the start.

If the police want to search you:

Tell them, "I do not consent to a search." They will probably search you anyway, but make sure you let them know any search they conduct is without your consent.

If the police disrespect you:

Do not disrespect the police. You may have a right to be disrespectful and feel the need to be disrespectful when they disrespect you, but do not. If you do, the police will most likely arrest you for some trumped-up charge.

If the police lie to you:

Do not lie to the police. In Indiana, like most states, it is against the law to lie to the police. In Indiana, it is often called false reporting. Instead, exercise your constitutional right to remain silent and request to speak with a criminal defense attorney. However, the police can legally lie to you and even intimidate you. If you want to know if the police can lie to you, the answer is YES!

CHAPTER 12

COMPASSIONATE RELEASE

18 U.S.C. 4205(g) was repealed effective November 1, 1987, but remains the controlling law for federal inmates whose offenses occurred before that date. For inmates whose offenses occurred on or after November 1, 1987, the applicable statute is 18 U.S.C. 3582(c)(1) (A). Procedures for compassionate release of a federal inmate under either provision are contained in 28 C.F.R. part 571, subpart G.

Because of the pandemic, petitions for compassionate release increased. The federal compassionate release is a formal request for a reduction in the sentence of a federal prisoner. In the federal criminal justice system, a petition for compassionate release was created by federal statute, pursuant to 18 U.S.C.A. § 3582(c)(1)(A), as modified by the First Step Act.

The compassionate release statute was first enacted as part of the Comprehensive Crime Control Act of 1984. It provided that a district court could not modify a final term of imprisonment, except in four situations, one of which was the existence of "extraordinary and compelling reasons," warranting the reduction as determined by the sentencing court. Although the courts had the final decision-making authority over whether a sentence would be reduced, the statute imposed the Director of the Federal Bureau of Prisons (B.O.P.) could invoke that authority only upon a motion. If the Director of the B.O.P. did not file the motion, sentencing courts could not reduce a prisoner's sentence, even if the court concluded that extraordinary and compelling reasons warranted the reduction. 18 U.S.C.A. § 3582(c)(1)(A)(i).

The statute created an expectation that if "extraordinary and compelling reasons" developed during a sentence, the court would have the opportunity to reduce the term of imprisonment after considering the factors outlined in section 3553(a) to the extent they are applicable. 18 U.S.C.A. § 3582(c)(1)(A)(I) (Section 3582(c)(1)(A)(I) allowed "in any case .

- . . the court, upon motion of the Director of the Bureau of Prisons, may reduce the [defendant's] term of imprisonment . . . after considering the factors outlined in section 3553(a) to the extent that they are applicable if it finds that . . . extraordinary and compelling reasons warrant such a reduction."). The expectation was that prisoners with serious illnesses would have their cases reviewed under the compassionate release statute.

In 2018, Congress limited the B.O.P.'s ability to impede compassionate release reviews. They amended the First Step Act to allow a court to sua sponte reduce a sentence for "extraordinary and compelling reasons" in two circumstances: (i) if the Director of the B.O.P. files a motion requesting such relief; or (ii) "upon motion of the defendant," if the defendant has fully exhausted all administrative remedies to appeal the B.O.P.'s failure to bring a motion, or if thirty days have lapsed "from the receipt of such a request by the warden of the defendant's facility," whichever is earlier. 18 U.S.C.A. § 3582(c)(1)(A). See,

United States v. Cantu, 423 F. Supp.3d 345 (S.D. Tex. 2019). Fortunately, Congress did not limit "extraordinary and compelling reasons" to a specific, enumerated set of circumstances. They did not define what would constitute an "extraordinary and compelling reason" warranting a reduction of a sentence under § 3582(c). Congress granted federal sentencing courts broad discretion to make those determinations on a case-by-case basis and to reduce fundamentally unfair sentences where such reasons exist.

Not a Danger to the Safety of Any Other Person or the Community

Compassionate release requires that the defendant not be a danger to the safety of any other person or the community and requires that the court considers the following factors when determining whether there are conditions of release that will reasonably assure the appearance of the person as required and the safety of any other person and the community:

(1) the nature and circumstances of the offense charged, including whether the offense is a crime of violence, a violation of section 1591, a federal crime of

terrorism, or involves a minor victim or a controlled substance, firearm, explosive, or destructive device;

(2) the weight of the evidence against the person;

(3) the history and characteristics of the person, including—

(A) the person's character, physical and mental condition, family ties, employment, financial resources, length of residence in the community, community ties, past conduct, history relating to drug or alcohol abuse, criminal history, and record concerning appearance at court proceedings, and

(B) whether, at the time of the current offense or arrest, the person was on probation, on parole, or other release pending trial, sentencing, appeal, or completion of sentence for an offense under federal, state, or local law; and

(4) the nature and seriousness of the danger to any person or the community that would be posed by the person's release.

Indiana Courts

In Indiana, there is currently not a compassionate release statute. However, during the pandemic, you could file a compassionate release motion, using some of the same language from the federal law to help get release.

CHAPTER 13

TORTS

A tort is a wrongful act or an infringement of a right (other than under contract) leading to civil legal liability. A court can provide a remedy in the form of damages. These cases always involve a violation of some duty owed to the person. There are three elements involved in torts:

1. There is a legal duty that the defendant owes to the claimant

2. A breach of that duty

3. Injury or damages as a proximate cause of the breach of the duty

In prisoner litigation, there are generally two types of torts:

1. Intentional torts, where a person intended to do what the law has said to be wrong. An example of an intentional tort is if a correctional officer (unjustifiably) intentionally broke a prisoner's leg.

2. Negligent tort, where a person was careless in their conduct. An example of a negligent tort is if a correctional officer acted carelessly or recklessly and broke a prisoner's leg. The guard may have failed to exercise the degree of care required by law.

In a civil tort case, they mainly limit the damages to money. There can be compensatory damages covering actual monetary loss; for example, medical or personal injuries or lost wages. There can be punitive damages to punish the defendant for severely bad conduct, and this requires a showing of gross negligence or recklessness or willful negligence.

In prison law, the most common tort involves the negligent loss of prisoners' property, medical malpractice, and battery.

CHAPTER 14

PRISON LITIGATION REFORM ACT

Constitution

As on the street, the most important source of rights for prisoners is the U.S. Constitution. The U.S. Supreme Court is the final interpreter of constitutional rights.

Section 1983 is the most common means for taking legal action against prison officials. This area of law was used to establish most of the constitutional rights of prisoners. It allows for a wider scope of judicial review and broader relief opportunities.

Prison Litigation Reform Act

The Prison Litigation Reform Act (PLRA) was signed into law in 1996 and is codified in 42 USC Section 1997(e). The PLRA requires prisoners to exhaust all their administrative remedies before suing concerning prison conditions under Section 1983 or any other federal law. It allows for dismissing frivolous, malicious, or ill-founded lawsuits without requiring exhaustion of administrative remedies. It limits attorney fees and prevents the filing of a federal civil action for mental or emotional injury while incarcerated without a prior showing of physical injury.

If the prisoner wants to proceed *in forma pauperis* (in the character or manner of a pauper), alleging they are without money to pay court fees and request the court to waive the fees, they need to submit documentation showing the lack of funds. PLRA limited court order relief from prison conditions and placed other limitations on the courts. The objective was not to reduce abuses in prison, but to reduce the volume of prison litigation. In that respect, the PLRA succeeded.

CHAPTER 15

SECTION 1983

1983

The Federal Civil Rights Act of 1871 codified in title 42 United States Code Section 1983 created Section 1983 lawsuits. These are often called constitutional torts and involve an injury or harm suffered by a person because of another's wrongful actions. It refers to injuries caused by a violation of rights guaranteed by the Constitution, which is the origin of the name of constitutional tort.

Since the 1960s, the most frequently used type of lawsuit in prison litigation was section 1983. Prisoners alleged state officials were violating their rights. Prisoners alleged the officials were acting under the color of state law and deprived them of their constitutional rights. Many state prisoners brought actions in federal courts, believing them to be more favorably disposed to litigation against prisons than state courts.

Section 1983 lawsuits allow both damages and injunctive relief. Damages refers to the amount of money the law allows for a breach of some duty or violation of a right.

Generally, there are two types of damages: compensatory and punitive. Compensatory damages are intended to compensate the injured party for a loss or an injury. Punitive damages are to punish the party that caused the injury.

Injunctive relief (an injunction) is a remedy restraining a party from committing certain acts or orders a party to do something. There are two main types of injunctions:

1. Restrictive injunctions, when defendants are legally ordered to stop what they are doing. An example of a restrictive injunction is ordering the prison to stop placing prisoners in solitary confinement without due process. The court could order the prison to stop what they are doing.

2. Mandatory injunctions are when defendants are required to do certain things. An example of a mandatory injunction is ordering the prison to release all the prisoners placed in solitary confinement without due process.

A prisoner's claim for damages may not be tried or examined under 1983 if a judgment for the prisoner would imply that the conviction or sentence was invalid. However, that is not the case if the conviction or sentence had already been invalidated. In those instances, habeas corpus would be the appropriate judicial remedy. If a prisoner believes their rights were violated to get a conviction, they usually cannot sue under section 1983. Section 1983 is not the proper remedy to challenge a conviction. The prisoner should challenge the conviction under habeas corpus.

A prisoner can sue if they believe their constitutional rights were violated. A section 1983 lawsuit is against the prison officials, not against the state or correctional facility. The person being sued must have operated under the color of state law. Basically, when a prisoner sues under 1983, it is against the offending official, for example, the warden or superintendent of the prison. Lawsuits under Section 1983 are against state officials.

Federal 1983

In *Bivens v. Six Unknown Federal Narcotics Agents,* 403 U.S. 388 (1971), the Supreme Court held federal officials could be sued for violating a person's constitutional rights. The *Bivens* case involved federal narcotics agents acting under a claim of federal authority, and they entered the petitioner's apartment without a warrant. They searched the apartment and arrested the petitioner on a narcotics charge. They had no probable cause. The petitioner sued, alleging unlawful arrest and asked for monetary damages from each of the agents. The lower courts ruled in favor of the government, stating the complaint failed to state a federal cause of action. At the time, Section 1983 only covered state officials. However, the United States Supreme Court would reverse that and ruled that the federal agents' actions violated the Fourth Amendment's bar against unreasonable search and seizure. This ruling created a federally protected interest. The United States Supreme Court in *Bivens* allowed a person to sue for constitutional civil rights violations by federal officials.

Under *Bivens,* citizens can sue for constitutional civil rights violations against federal officials in the same manner as Congress allowed lawsuits against state officials in Section 1983. An important aspect of both Section 1983 and *Bivens* is a judgment that the individual defendant must pay any monetary award from their private financial resources. However, the government may still represent the defendant and often does. If the individual defendant is held liable, the government may indemnify (or protect) the defendant.

CHAPTER 16

RESTRICTIONS AND LEGAL ASSISTANCE

Constitutional Restrictions

Restrictions on a prisoner's constitutional rights are allowed if they are reasonably related to legitimate penological interests. In *Turner v. Safley*, 482 U.S. 78 (1987), the Supreme Court held that prison regulations related to a legitimate penological interest would generally be upheld. Therefore, if prisoners cannot show a prison regulation unrelated to a legitimate penological interest, the courts will generally uphold the restriction as not violating the prisoner's constitutional rights.

Legal Assistance

States must protect prisoners' right to access courts by providing law libraries or an alternative legal information source. In *Bounds v. Smith*, 430 U.S. 817 (1977), the Supreme Court held that the "fundamental constitutional right of access to the courts requires prison authorities to assist inmates by providing prisoners with adequate law libraries or adequate assistance from" people trained in the law to help in filing meaningful legal documents. However, law libraries are not constitutionally required if there is an alternative means of adequate legal assistance. The States (prisons) can decide the means of assistance. Also, *Bounds* guaranteed prisoners' access to the courts to file habeas corpus and other civil rights complaints under Section 1983.

Unfortunately, like most prison litigation areas, in 1996, the Supreme Court would limit

Bounds. In *Lewis v. Casey*, 518 U.S. 343 (1996), the Supreme Court criticized the lower court for not deferring to the prison officials' judgment regarding the type of law library and other legal assistance offered to prisoners. The Supreme Court held that a prisoner's right to access the court encompassed: Direct appeals from their convictions, habeas corpus actions, and Section 1983 lawsuits. The only required assistance was for the initial preparation and filing, not for litigating the case to the end.

Although the Supreme Court did not officially overrule *Bounds*, it limited it and emphasized the importance of deferring to prison officials.

No Constitutional Right to Post-Conviction Counsel

Prisoners do not have a constitutional right to counsel for collateral attacks on their sentences, even in death penalty cases. In *Murry v. Giarratano*, 492 U.S. 1 (1989), the Supreme Court held that neither the Eighth Amendment nor due process clause requires states to appoint counsel for indigent death-row inmates seeking state Post- Conviction Relief. When prisoners have counsel, prison officials must balance the prison's need for legitimate oversight of prisoner activities for the safety and security of the prison, the attorney and client needs, and allow for protected opportunities for communications by phone, visits and mail.

Public Defender of Indiana

Indiana provides a limited right to Post-Conviction Relief counsel under Ind. Post- Conviction Rule 1(9). In 1969, the Indiana Supreme Court adopted this rule, creating the Public Defender of Indiana. A judicial branch agency is the Public Defender of Indiana. The Supreme Court appoints the State Public Defender, and the person serves at the pleasure of the Indiana Supreme Court. The primary purpose is to ensure fairness in criminal proceedings by assisting in Post-Conviction Remedies.

The agency provides Post-Conviction Relief (PCR) factual and legal investigations and representation at the hearing and appeal in all indigent prisoners' capital cases. In noncapital cases, an investigation occurs after the indigent prisoner files a pro se petition for Post-Conviction Relief. The trial court will appoint the State Public Defender Office to represent the incarcerated indigent petitioner. They provide representation at a PCR hearing and on appeal when the case has arguable merit. However, if the petitioner is not incarcerated, the State Public Defender may refuse to represent the petitioner. Because of budgetary restrictions, the State Public Defender's primary focus is on those incarcerated or facing penal consequences.

Limiting Access to Courts

Prisoners have a right to access the courts, but there are consequences if they abuse that right. Some examples under PLRA are prisoners may have to pay filing fees, their case may be dismissed, and there is a "Three Strikes" rule. The Three Strikes Rule prevents a prisoner from filing a federal civil rights lawsuit as a pauper or filing future lawsuits as a pauper unless under imminent threat of serious physical injury. The Three Strikes rule occurs when the record shows three previous lawsuits dismissed as frivolous, malicious, failing to state a claim upon which relief may be granted, or seeking monetary relief from a defendant entitled to immunity from such relief.

Chapter 17

Jail/Prison Phone Calls

Another area that causes concern is talking on the phone. I always advise clients that are incarcerated to not talk about their case on the phone. Do not speak to family, friends, or anybody about the case over the prison or jail phone. You should communicate with the mindset that everything you say is being recorded and everything you write is being read.

Prosecutors love to listen to jail calls. The phone calls are recorded, and the jail/prison officials or prosecutor will use the calls against you. I have seen a winning case become a losing case because the accused talked on the phone about the crime, admitting guilt, planning to lie, trying to get other people to lie, threatening witnesses, and even talking about the defense attorney's trial strategy.

Courts have ruled that jail does not have the same attributes as a home, car, office, or even a hotel room. Jail and prison officials have a justifiable safety and security concern in monitoring and recording phone conversations. *Lanza v. New York*, 370 US 139 (1962) and

United States v. Hearst, 563 F.2d 1331(1977). Under the federal wiretapping statute, prison officials may record prisoner conversations within the ordinary course of business, to monitor prison phone calls, and without prior judicial approval. It allows for the monitoring of phone calls with the consent of one party involved in the conversation.

Most prisons and jails today have warnings that phone calls are being recorded and monitored. Yet, people make incriminating statements and then act surprised when their own words are used against them.

Fortunately, there are legal protections for attorney-client conversations. It is ethically and legally improper for prison officials to listen in and record attorney-client conversations. Unfortunately, it can and does happen.

CHAPTER 18

PRISONER'S SILENCE

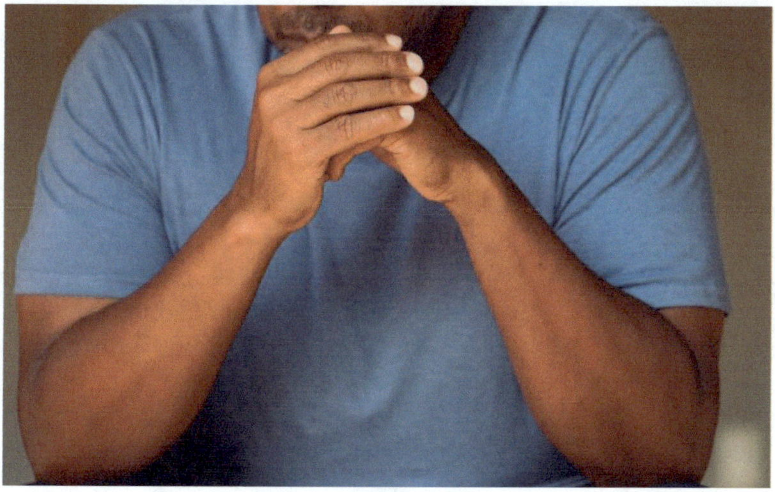

In *Baxter v. Palmigiano*, 425 U.S. 308 (1976), the Supreme Court held prisoners could be advised that their silence can be used against them during prisoner disciplinary proceedings, but that alone is not enough to determine that the prisoner is engaged in the conduct. In other words, prisoners cannot be convicted by their silence alone; there needs to be additional evidence. In prison, the burden of proof to find someone guilty is not "beyond a reasonable doubt." Essentially, the standard to find that a prisoner violated the rules is "some evidence." See, *Superintendent v. Hill*, 472 U.S. 445 (1985). If the conduct rises to the level of a crime, then an additional procedure must take place. If they ordered the prisoner to testify, they must give the prisoner immunity from the use of that testimony in a later criminal proceeding.

On the street, a person's silence cannot be used against them. If a person confesses to a crime, the confession alone cannot convict them. There has to be something more. In law, the phrase "corpus delicti" is used, meaning the body of the crime. There must be some concrete evidence that a crime occurred other than the person just saying they committed a crime.

CHAPTER 19

OVERVIEW OF THE FEDERAL RIGHTS

Below, I summarize federal rights as it applies to prisoners. It does not address the various state constitutions.

A "right" may be defined as a moral or legal entitlement to have or get something or act in a certain way or something to which one is justly entitled.

The Bill of Rights is the first ten amendments to the U.S. Constitution. I heard them called a Bill of Privileges since all of them can be taken away by the government. Are they even rights if they can be taken away from you? Are they absolute rights when they are not equally applied to all? All that sounds like privileges. For example, our government can take away your freedom by sending you to prison, taking your kids through termination of parental rights, violating your privacy by monitoring your phone calls and emails and can even take your life by using the death penalty. Prison officials abuse the use of solitary confinement, a form of torture, despite the Eighth Amendment.

Prisoners have certain rights—like the right to send and receive letters, make phone calls, attend religious services and meetings, and access the law library. But these are all "conditional" rights. They are rights only if the government allows you to exercise them. If not, you do not have the right. It is the same for due process. If the government holds hearings and gives you due process, then you get to have those hearings. If not, you do not. Due process is essential because it protects against the abuses of power by government officials. When those in power can get away with taking away your rights without providing you with any kind of process, it makes a mockery of our legal system and society.

U.S. military personnel tortured the detainees at Abu Ghraib prison that were suspected of terrorism. Our country held people for years without charges at the U.S. military prison in Guantanamo Bay, Cuba. What do you think they think of our legal system? Or what do you think the over two million prisoners held in state and federal prisons and jails here in the United States think about our legal system? The people that were wrongfully convicted probably think justice delayed is justice denied.

First Amendment

Freedom of Speech: This right protects speech and the ability to send and receive correspondence and access to reading materials, such as books. There are many restrictions on books, magazines, letters, and prison mail.

No rights are absolute, and the First Amendment rights are no exception.

Press: The media has no more rights than an average citizen to access prisons or prisoners.

Assembly: The United States Supreme Court held prison officials could bar prisoners from unionizing. Prison officials often use anti-gang policies to prohibit “assembly” and place prisoners in long-term solitary confinement. They will use the language that they know will please the courts by stating it is for the “safety and security” of the prison.

Religion: Prisoners keep some religious rights. The Religious Land Use and Institutionalized Persons Act (RLUIPA) does not provide damages, just injunctive relief.

Petition for redress of grievances: The Prison Litigation Reform Act (PLRA) requires exhaustion of "available" grievance procedures. Prison officials usually frustrate that process. The law does not require a formal grievance procedure. However, most jails and prisons have a formal grievance procedure. Grievances are gatekeepers to federal litigation, and sometimes a grievance-filing deadline will effectively evade (or miss) the statute of limitations to sue in federal court. The rules and procedures for grievances are complicated for prisoners who are illiterate or have mental health issues. The basic purpose of a grievance process is for prisoners and prison staff to try and resolve concerns and complaints relating to their conditions of confinement. This is an internal prison policy and procedure that does not require outside court intervention.

Unfortunately, when prisoners file a grievance, they risk being retaliated against by prison officials. In theory, retaliation for valid grievances is prohibited. The standard legal claim for retaliation is an adverse action that deters prisoners of "ordinary firmness" from exercising their rights. What is "ordinary firmness?" The courts have not explicitly defined it.

Access to the courts: The Supreme Court has limited this right in the landmark case of *Lewis v. Casey*, that I mentioned previously. Prisoners that file a claim that they are being denied access to the courts must show actual injury to a current case or anticipated litigation. Any claim that alleges a denial of that right must show the current or anticipated litigation is not frivolous.

Second Amendment

Under the Second Amendment, there is a right to own firearms. A collateral consequence of a felony conviction is the prohibition on gun ownership. There are federal and similar state laws against convicted felons in possession of firearms.

Third Amendment

"No Soldier shall, in time of peace, be quartered in any house, without the consent of the Owner, nor in time of war, but in a manner to be prescribed by law." I mentioned this because I am not aware of this right being restricted or violated in the last twenty years or more. The United States Supreme Court mentioned it in *Griswold v. Connecticut*, 381 U.S. 479 (1965). The next famous case was in 1982 *Engblom v. Carey* decision by the U.S.

Court of Appeals for the Second Circuit. The court found that the state of New York violated the rights of striking correctional officers by quartering National Guard troops in the state-owned homes from which the officers had been evicted.

Fourth Amendment

Prisoners do not have a reasonable expectation of privacy in their cells, so they can be searched at will. They can be strip-searched. They are subject to random drug tests and pat-down searches.

There are some Fourth Amendment protections, such as against unjustified body cavity searches, group strip searches, or strip searches in front of people of the opposite gender, except in exigent circumstances.

The law allows prison and jail officials to search visitors. They mainly strip search visitors when there is reasonable suspicion of criminal conduct.

Fifth Amendment

Double jeopardy does not apply to prison disciplinary hearings and criminal prosecutions; prisoners can face criminal charges and prison discipline for the same conduct.

While prisoners can exercise their right against self-incrimination at parole hearings, that is likely to result in denial of parole when parole officials ask about details related to their crimes (which may still be on appeal).

The Fifth Amendment's prohibition on "private property . . . taken for public use, without just compensation" becomes almost meaningless in the face of civil forfeiture laws. Civil forfeiture, which involves seizing private property even in the absence of criminal charges, has resulted in widespread abuse and misconduct by law enforcement agencies. A recent U.S. Supreme Court decision hopefully slowed down some of the abuse. See, *Timbs v. Indiana*, 139 S. Ct. 682 (2019).

Sixth Amendment

This Amendment ensures the assistance of counsel. Unfortunately, there are still cases where people can receive jail time but are not provided attorneys if they cannot afford one. For example, child support, contempt of court, and probation violations, just to name a few. However, in Indiana, in most cases, if the person is accused of violating the terms of probation, they will be appointed an attorney if they are found indigent.

There is no right to counsel at prison disciplinary hearings. If an attorney attends, the attorney usually cannot participate or even speak. They are relegated to the role of an observer.

Eighth Amendment

A component of the Eighth Amendment is a prohibition on excessive bail. This prohibits cruel and unusual punishment. Also, it prohibits excessive fines. In prison, the most common claim brought under this Amendment usually involves failure to treat prisoners' medical or mental health needs properly. However, it prohibits excessive force and requires prison officials to protect prisoners from harm.

Thirteenth Amendment

Slavery is constitutional in the United States. The Thirteenth Amendment did not abolish slavery. If you are convicted of a crime and sent to prison, you will be a slave to the government. I quote from the Amendment, "Neither slavery nor involuntary servitude, except as a punishment for crime whereof the party shall have been duly convicted, shall exist within the United States, or any place subject to their jurisdiction."

This Amendment is a racist reminder of the Black Codes and Jim Crow Laws of the past. Prisoners are modern-day slaves, and prisons are the plantations. Most prisoners are paid meager wages, if any at all. Prison officials can force prisoners to work and punish them if they do not.

Fourteenth Amendment

Due process rights involving prisoners are most often raised in prison disciplinary hearings.

Unfortunately, the U.S. Supreme Court gutted due process for prison disciplinary hearings. There are very few cases that rise to the level of an "atypical and significant hardship."

Voting Rights: Disenfranchisement

In most states, you cannot vote while in prison. Currently, there are only two states that allow prisoners to vote while incarcerated: Maine and Vermont. Some states allow people on probation or parole to vote, while others do not. Only one state permanently disenfranchises people with a felony conviction: Virginia.

Unfortunately, the U.S. Supreme Court upheld the disenfranchisement of ex-felons in *Richardson v. Ramirez*, 418 U.S. (1974).

CHAPTER 20

KNOW YOUR RIGHTS

Why Is It Important to Know My Rights?

When people are not aware of their rights, the government can take advantage of them. Mostly, the government has limitless resources and access to some of the world's best experts and people. If you do not know your rights, it is easier for them to violate your rights. The government can use its vast resources to prosecute someone that is innocent. When there is no case, the government can use its resources to create a case. The more that you do not know about the law and your constitutional rights, the easier it is for the government to violate those sacred rights. There is no more significant threat than the government abusing its authority. If an individual sues you, you are more or less on equal footing with them. But when the government comes after you, they usually have more resources than you do. You do not want to think that you are helping your case when you are hurting it because you don't know your rights.

Why Do Your Experiences Make You Unique?

I had the unfortunate experience of serving two places that people fear the most: combat and prison. By the grace of God, I survived both. I do not say that rhetorically. God has helped me and continues to help me in life. I am not perfect, never claimed to be, but I know that my faith in God has inspired me and, hopefully, will inspire others.

I know what it is like in prison and on the street, and I take my cases seriously. I do not want to forget that it could be me or one of my loved ones. In each case that I have, I look at it as though I am the client, understanding that I was in their shoes. How would I want to be treated in that situation? Because of my experience, I will never forget what it is like on the other side. I am a dedicated fighter for my clients. I became an attorney to fight against a travesty of justice, and that is what I do. The motto of my law firm is we are a people-helping law firm and we are in the business of helping people.

CHAPTER 21

MY HOPE

I hope this short book motivates you to believe that you can successfully navigate the many challenges in the prison system or on the street. Perhaps this book gave you a nugget of knowledge you did not know before. At some point, I plan to publish my memoir, which will go into a lot more detail about the experiences I faced while being incarcerated, being homeless, attending law school, and becoming an attorney. In the meantime, please subscribe to my newsletter, *The*

Nicholson Nugget, for updates on legal issues, other book releases, and a chance to win prizes.

You can subscribe to *The Nicholson Nugget* at: https://www.marknicholsonlaw.com/blog or visit my website https://www.marknicholsonlaw.com/

Here are links to a few of my blog posts.

https://www.marknicholsonlaw.com/criminal-law/domestic-violence

https://www.marknicholsonlaw.com/criminal-law/ovwi-dui/stopped-for-a-dui-ovwi

https://www.marknicholsonlaw.com/what-is-qualified-immunity-should-it-be-reformed

NOTES

The acronym for my law firm's core values spells HELPER.

H: Honesty

E: Excellence

L: Loyalty

P: Passion

E: Earn

R: Respect

WHAT IS THE NEXT STEP?

Know your rights, and if you see someone needing help, please help them if you can. People helped me when I was in need; now, I'm trying to help others in need.

Please visit my website for more information at marknicholsonlaw.com or call me at 317-667-0718.

By: Mark Nicholson

Made in United States
Cleveland, OH
20 August 2025

19587136R00081